Rose Elliot's Book of Pasta

Rose Elliot is the author of several bestselling cookbooks, and is renowned for her practical and creative approach. She writes regularly for the *Vegetarian* and has contributed to national newspapers and magazines as well as broadcasting on radio and television. She is married and has three children.

D0716012

Other titles available in the series

Rose Elliot's Book of

Pasta

Fontana Paperbacks

First published by Fontana Paperbacks 1984

Set in 10 on 11pt Linotron Plantin
Drawings by Vana Haggerty
except pages 8–9, 12, 14 and 44 by Ken Lewis
Made and printed in Great Britain by
William Collins Sons & Co. Ltd, Glasgow

Introduction

Cheap to buy, convenient to store and fast to cook, pasta can be made into some of the most satisfying dishes, ranging from homely macaroni cheese to delicious spaghetti with aubergine and red wine, lasagne with Cheddar cheese and walnuts, and tagliatelle with creamy mushroom sauce. Pasta meals invariably bring an atmosphere of particular warmth and relaxed conviviality, especially when served with some inexpensive Italian wine which adds the finishing touch.

At only 200 calories a serving (175 g/6 oz cooked weight), pasta is not nearly as high in calories as many people believe. It can be enjoyed by slimmers and weight watchers as long as more fattening accompaniments, such as cream, butter and cheese, are used with discretion.

Pasta is made from a dough of hard wheat flour which is rolled and pushed through nozzles to form various shapes, then dried. If the dough is made with water, the pasta is called pasta secco; if egg is used, it is called pasta all'uovo. Pasta all'uovo can be bought dried and also freshly made, undried. It is possible to make excellent pasta all'uovo at home: see pages 11–13. Sometimes pasta dough is flavoured with spinach to make the green pasta verde, and an increasing range of shapes are becoming available in a wholewheat version of pasta.

One of the attractions of pasta is the large variety of charming shapes in which it is made. There are scores of these, often with amusingly descriptive names. Here is a list of some of the most popular and widely available:

1 Anelli Pasta rings, especially good in salads and savoury bakes. The wholewheat version is particularly good and my favourite type of wholewheat pasta.

2 Cannelloni Large pasta tubes. Par-boiled, then filled with stuffing, such as the curd cheese stuffing on page 22 or the walnut, tomato and red wine stuffing on page 24, and baked in a tasty sauce, these make a delicious dish.

3 Conchiglie Shells, available in various shapes and sizes. Delicious with olive oil, garlic and fresh herbs, or mixed with colourful vegetables as in the recipe for hot conchiglie with avocado and mozzarella cheese (page 25); conchiglie with red and white beans in parsley butter (page 27); and conchiglie salad with cucumber, nuts and raisins in curried mayonnaise (page 28).

4 Farfalle Butterflies. Good as above, with butter or olive oil and grated cheese, or mixed with vegetables as in the recipe for farfalle with courgettes, peas and mint (page 31), or farfalle with mushrooms and parsley (page 29).

5 Fettucce A wide, ribbon-like egg noodle. Fettuccine is a narrower version. Both are excellent with creamy sauces.

6 Lasagne Broad strips of pasta which are cooked and then rolled round tasty ingredients, or layered with them in an ovenproof dish and baked, as in lasagne with aubergine, onions and tomatoes (page 32); lasagne, red kidney bean and wine bake (page 35), and lasagne with spinach and curd cheese (page 36). Some people do not cook lasagne first and add extra liquid to the dish to compensate, and you can buy lasagne specially prepared for using like this. This saves time, but I do not think the results are as light and good as when using freshly cooked lasagne.

7 Linguini Flat spaghetti; use like spaghetti (see below).

8 Maccheroni Macaroni. Can be bought in straight or curved 'elbow' versions, and in varying thicknesses, some with ridges. Serve with tasty sauces, like the very easy one in the recipe for macaroni with four cheeses on page 40; with cooked vegetables (see recipe for macaroni with butter beans, tomatoes and black olives, page 38), or in salad mixtures, like the one on page 41.

9 Penne Straight macaroni with diagonally cut ends, like the nib of a pen. Use like macaroni.

10 Ravioli Little cushions of pasta containing a filling; they are cooked and served with butter and grated cheese, or with a sauce. Specially good when homemade, with your own choice of filling, as in the recipes on pages 43 and 45.

11 Rigatone Large, ridged pasta tubes, generally served in a sauce or in baked dishes. The ridges help the sauce to cling to the pasta.

12 Ruote di carro Cartwheels, good with a sauce, popular with children, especially when served with the tomato sauce on page 51 and sprinkled with grated cheese.

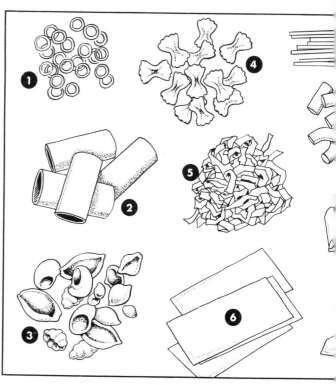

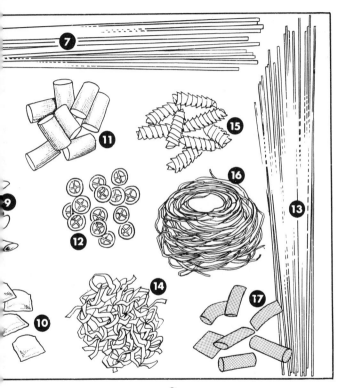

13 Spaghetti Probably the best known and most popular type of pasta. Makes an excellent quick meal when served with a tasty sauce, such as the mushroom cream sauce (page 49); the lentil and red wine sauce (page 48), or the classic rich green pesto (page 50).

14 Tagliatelle Ribbon-like egg noodles, usually coiled into bundles before packing. Can be used like spaghetti; particularly good with creamy sauces such as the easy cheese sauce on page 52 and the walnut sauce on page 56.

15 Tortiglioni Pasta spirals, like little corkscrews. Look pretty when mixed with colourful vegetables and in salads, as in tortiglioni salad with avocado (page 57).

16 Vermicelli Thin spaghetti, usually packed in coils. Cooks very quickly; ideal in delicate vegetable mixtures, such as the recipe for vermicelli with young carrots, broad beans and summer savory on page 59, or the classic dish *tuoni e lampo*, vermicelli with chick peas and garlic (page 61).

17 Wholewheat pasta Many of the above shapes can now be bought in a healthy wholewheat version, and the range is expanding. Wholewheat pasta looks quite dark in the packet, but is lighter after cooking. It has a delicious nutty flavour but is a little heavier than white pasta. All the recipes in this book can be made with either white or wholewheat pasta: the choice is yours, but where I think a wholewheat pasta gives a particularly good result, I have specified this in the ingredients.

HOW TO MAKE YOUR OWN PASTA

If you enjoy pasta and eat a fair amount of it, you might find it worthwhile making your own at home. Using one of the new pasta machines makes it a surprisingly quick and easy process; it's fun to do, and the results are very good.

EQUIPMENT

You'll need a large bowl for mixing the dough, a pastry wheel if you want to make ravioli (see page 44), and a pasta-making machine. You can buy electric pasta machines, also fitments for some electric mixers, but I think the little hand machines are best for normal domestic use. These consist of rollers which are turned by a handle, like an old fashioned mangle, and are easy both to use and to clean.

INGREDIENTS

To make 175 g (6 oz) pasta you will need:

100 g (3½ oz) plain flour: wholewheat, wheatmeal, unbleached white, or a mixture. Bread flour, made from hard wheat, is best.

¼ teaspoon salt

1 egg, size 3

METHOD

Put the flour and salt into a bowl and crack in the egg. Using your hands, mix the flour, little by little, into the egg, until you have a fairly smooth dough.

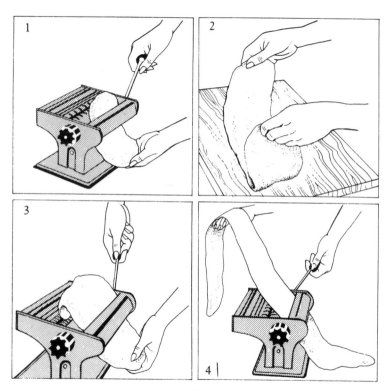

12

Set the rollers of your pasta machine to their widest position. Take a piece of pasta dough about the size of an egg, flatten it roughly with your hands, then feed it through the rollers (see figure 1 on page 12). Fold the piece of dough in three, as shown in figure 2 (page 12), then feed it through again.

Do this six or seven times, until the dough is smooth and pliable, then lay it on one side and repeat the process with the rest of the dough, keeping the pieces in the right order.

Next, tighten the rollers a notch and put the pieces of pasta through again, once only this time, and without folding. Repeat three times, tightening the rollers a notch each time. Cut the pieces of pasta in half if they become too long to handle, and support them as they come through the machine so that they don't fall in folds and stick together.

If you want to make lasagne, cannelloni or ravioli, feed the pasta through the machine again with the rollers on the tightest setting but one. The pasta can then be cut to the required size and used straight away in savoury bakes, without further drying or cooking. For ravioli, see page 44. If you want to make noodles, pass the sheets of pasta through one of the cutting rollers, then spread it out on a clean, lightly floured cloth, or drape it over the edge of a saucepan or clean piece of dowelling or broom handle, and leave it to dry for 1 hour. It can then be cooked as described below, allowing 2–3 minutes only.

Fresh pasta can replace the same quantity of dried pasta in any recipe. Like dried pasta, fresh pasta will swell and expand as it cooks.

HOW TO COOK PASTA

Allow 25–50 g (1–2 oz) uncooked pasta for each person for a first course; 75–125 g (3–4 oz) per person for a main course.

Pasta needs to be cooked in plenty of water to enable it to move around and thus not stick together. Allow 1.1 litre (2 pints) water for every 125 g (4 oz) pasta, or 4 litres (6 pints) for 500 g (1 lb). Put the water into a large saucepan, or two smaller ones if necessary, and add a teaspoonful of salt. You can also add a tablespoonful of oil, if you like: this helps prevent the pasta from sticking together. Bring the water to the boil.

When the water reaches boiling point, add the pasta. Long types like spaghetti need to be eased into the water. Hold the spaghetti like a bunch of flowers, stand it upright in the water and gradually let it all down into the water as it softens and bends: see page 14. Drop other types of pasta into the water a few at a time, then give them a stir once they're all in. Let the pasta boil gently, without a lid on the pan.

It's important not to overcook pasta. It should be tender but not

15

soggy. Most packets state a cooking time, but it's best to treat this as a guide only, and to start testing the pasta well before that time is up. To see if pasta is cooked, take a piece out of the water and bite it. It should be tender yet still have a little resistance: *al dente* – 'to the tooth' as Italians say. If it's not quite ready, cook it for a bit longer, but keep testing. Here is a very rough guide to the cooking times of various types of pasta:

very thin pasta, small shapes	5–9 minutes
larger shapes, long tubes	10–20 minutes
fresh pasta	2–3 minutes

As soon as the pasta is done, tip it into a colander to drain. Give it a shake, then put it back into the saucepan or into a heated serving dish with a knob of butter or some olive oil and salt and freshly ground black pepper to taste.

SERVING PASTA

Cooked pasta can be served simply, just with butter or olive oil and seasoning, and perhaps the addition of some crushed garlic or chopped fresh herbs, or a sprinkling of grated Parmesan cheese. Like this it's delicious as a first course, or even, with a colourful salad and extra grated cheese, as a simple main course: a great favourite with my young daughter and her friends.

For more luxurious mixtures, cream, curd cheese and other creamy cheeses can be added to the pasta in the saucepan, stirred briefly over the heat, then served. The two tagliatelle recipes, on pages 52 and 56, and maccheroni with four cheeses, page 40, are examples of this; they are also fast to make, and wonderful with a simple green salad for a supper that's quick, yet a bit special.

More elaborate sauces can be made separately, then served with the pasta. Some, like the mushroom sauce on page 49, can be made while the pasta is cooking; others, such as the sweet pepper sauce on page 55, need to be started a little beforehand to give them time to cook.

Cooked pasta is also good mixed with other cooked ingredients, particularly vegetables, which add colour to the dish. There are a number of recipes for such combinations in this book, and also for salads, which are made on the same principle, with cooked pasta being mixed with raw fruit and vegetables – filling, yet refreshing.

I think the pasta dishes I like making best are the baked ones: lasagne layered with tasty mixtures of vegetables, pulses and wine, then baked in a cheese sauce (page 35); cannelloni filled with a tasty stuffing and baked in a fresh tomato sauce (page 22), or the pretty and unusual anelli and aubergine loaf on page 19. There's plenty of scope for creativity.

Anelli and Aubergine Mould

An attractive and unusual first course or light lunch or supper dish.

SERVES 4–6

450 g (1 lb) aubergines
salt
4–6 tablespoons oil
2 onions, chopped
75 g (3 oz) anelli – wholewheat
   pasta rings
3 tomatoes, peeled and chopped

1 tablespoon tomato ketchup
1 teaspoon oregano
1 egg, beaten
freshly ground black pepper
grated Parmesan cheese, parsley
   sprig, to serve

Peel, slice, salt, fry and drain the aubergines as on page 32. Fry onions in 2 tablespoons of the oil for 10 minutes. Cook pasta in plenty of boiling salted water until just tender, drain and mix with onion, tomatoes, ketchup, oregano, egg and seasoning. Set oven to 200°C (400°F), gas mark 6. Put aubergine slices in base and sides of a well-buttered 450-g (1-lb) loaf tin. Spoon pasta mixture on top. Bake for 40–45 minutes. Turn out on to warmed plate, sprinkle with Parmesan, top with parsley.

Anelli and Carrot Salad
with Walnut Dressing

A particular favourite; the blend of colours and textures is just right. It's rich in protein and makes a complete light main course. If you can't get walnut oil, olive oil can be used instead.

SERVES 4

175 g (6 oz) anelli – wholewheat
   pasta rings
salt
3 tablespoons walnut oil
1 tablespoon wine vinegar

freshly ground black pepper
225 g (8 oz) grated carrot
125 g (4 oz) chopped walnuts
125 g (4 oz) chopped dates
small bunch watercress, to serve

Cook the anelli in plenty of boiling salted water until it's just tender; drain. Put the oil and vinegar into a bowl together with some salt and pepper; mix well, then add the pasta, carrot, walnuts and dates. Mix gently, until everything is well distributed and coated with the dressing. Heap up on a serving dish, tuck the watercress all round the edge to make a bright green border.

Anelli Savoury Bake

A quick, cheap and tasty dish that's good served with a cooked green vegetable.

SERVES 4

125 g (4 oz) anelli – wholewheat pasta rings
salt
2 onions, chopped
2 tablespoons oil
125 g (4 oz) mushrooms, chopped

225 g (8 oz) tomatoes, peeled and chopped
1 egg, beaten
125 g (4 oz) grated cheese
freshly ground black pepper
wholewheat breadcrumbs for topping

Set oven to 200°C (400°F), gas mark 6. Cook pasta in plenty of boiling salted water until just tender, drain and leave on one side. Fry onions in oil for 7 minutes, add mushrooms and tomatoes and fry for a further 3 minutes. Add egg and stir for a moment or two longer. Then remove from heat, add pasta rings, two-thirds of grated cheese and seasoning to taste. Put mixture into a lightly greased shallow ovenproof dish, sprinkle with breadcrumbs and rest of cheese and bake for 30 minutes.

Cannelloni filled with Curd Cheese and Baked in Tomato Sauce

You can use cannelloni or large squares of lasagne or homemade pasta for this recipe, which is good served with buttered spinach or broccoli or a watercress salad for a pretty colour contrast.

SERVES 4

12 cannelloni tubes or large
  squares of pasta
salt
225 g (8 oz) curd cheese

1 garlic clove, crushed
2 tablespoons milk
freshly ground black pepper
tomato sauce, page 51

Plunge pasta into boiling salted water: cook cannelloni for 4–5 minutes only, until pliable but not collapsed, lasagne or pasta squares until just tender. Drain well, spread out on clean cloth. Set oven to 200C° (400°F), gas mark 6. Mix curd cheese with garlic, milk and seasoning. Spoon curd cheese mixture into cannelloni, or spoon on top of pasta squares then make into rolls. Place in a greased shallow ovenproof dish, cover with sauce and bake for 45 minutes.

Cannelloni with Mushroom Stuffing Baked in Soured Cream

SERVES 4

12 cannelloni tubes or squares of
    pasta – see previous recipe
salt
1 onion, chopped
25 g (1 oz) butter
350 g (12 oz) mushrooms,
    chopped

1 garlic clove, crushed
50 g (2 oz) fine breadcrumbs
2 tablespoons chopped parsley
freshly ground black pepper
300 ml (11 fl oz) soured cream

Cook pasta as described in previous recipe, drain, spread out on a clean cloth and leave on one side. Set oven to 200°C (400°F), gas mark 6. Fry onion in butter for 5 minutes; add mushrooms and garlic and fry for 5 minutes more. If mushrooms make much liquid, increase heat and boil hard until this has gone. Remove from heat, add breadcrumbs, parsley and seasoning. Spoon into cannelloni, or on top of pasta squares then make into rolls. Place in a greased shallow ovenproof dish, cover with soured cream. Bake for 45 minutes.

Cannelloni with Walnuts, Tomatoes and Red Wine

Serve with the remaining wine for an excellent supper.

SERVES 4

12 cannelloni tubes or large
   squares of pasta, see page 9
salt
1 onion, peeled and chopped
1 garlic clove, crushed
2 tablespoons oil
225 g (8 oz) tomatoes, skinned
   and chopped

175 g (6 oz) walnuts, chopped
175 g (6 oz) fine wholewheat
   breadcrumbs
1 teaspoon basil
150 ml (5 fl oz) red wine
freshly ground black pepper
575 ml (1 pint) cheese sauce as
   on page 36

Cook pasta as described on page 22. Set oven to 200°C (400°F), gas mark 6. Fry onion and garlic in oil for 10 minutes, remove from heat, add tomatoes, walnuts, breadcrumbs, basil, wine and seasoning. Spoon mixture into cannelloni, or put on top of pasta squares then make into rolls. Place in a greased shallow ovenproof dish, cover with cheese sauce. Bake for 45 minutes.

Hot Conchiglie with Avocado and Mozzarella Cheese

Excellent as a hot first course or light supper dish.

SERVES 4—6

225–350 g (8–12 oz) conchiglie – pasta shells
salt
2 large avocado pears
2 tablespoons lemon juice
175 g (6 oz) mozzarella cheese
2 tablespoons olive oil
2 garlic cloves, crushed
2 tablespoons chopped parsley
freshly ground black pepper
grated Parmesan cheese, to serve

Cook pasta in plenty of boiling salted water until just tender, drain thoroughly. While pasta is cooking, halve avocados, remove stones and skins, dice flesh, sprinkle with lemon juice. Dice cheese. Add oil, garlic, parsley, avocado and cheese to hot drained pasta, stirring gently over the heat to distribute the ingredients and warm through the avocado and cheese. Grind in some black pepper to taste, then serve immediately. It's good with some grated Parmesan sprinkled over the top.

Conchiglie with Red and White Beans in Parsley Butter

This complements a salad with a creamy dressing, such as equal parts chopped celery and sweet apple bound with mayonnaise and natural yoghurt.

SERVES 4–6

225–350 g (8–12 oz) conchiglie – pasta shells
salt
40 g (1½ oz) butter
3 tablespoons chopped parsley
2 tablespoons lemon juice
125 g (4 oz) red kidney beans, soaked and cooked, or a 425–g (15–oz) can
125 g (4 oz) cannellini beans, soaked and cooked, or a 425–g (15–oz) can
freshly ground black pepper

Cook pasta in plenty of boiling salted water until just tender, drain thoroughly. While pasta is cooking, beat butter with parsley and lemon juice until well blended; leave on one side. Drain beans. Add parsley butter and beans to hot drained pasta and season. Stir gently over the heat until ingredients are well distributed and beans heated through. Serve immediately.

Conchiglie Salad with Cucumber, Nuts and Raisins in Curried Mayonnaise

A delicious blend of flavours and textures.

SERVES 4

½ cucumber
salt
225 g (8 oz) conchiglie – pasta shells
2 tablespoons mayonnaise
4 tablespoons natural yoghurt

1 teaspoon curry paste
50 g (2 oz) raisins
freshly ground black pepper
50 g (2 oz) flaked almonds, toasted
crisp lettuce leaves

Cut cucumber into 6-mm (¼-in) dice, sprinkle with salt, put into a colander under a weight and leave for 30 minutes, to draw off excess liquid, then pat dry with kitchen paper. Cook pasta in plenty of boiling salted water until just tender; drain thoroughly. In a large bowl mix together the mayonnaise, yoghurt and curry paste; add pasta, cucumber and raisins. Mix well, season to taste. Just before serving stir in most of the almonds; arrange lettuce leaves on serving dish, spoon salad on top, sprinkle with remaining nuts.

Farfalle with Mushrooms and Parsley

Serve with a tomato and watercress salad for a light supper dish.

SERVES 4–6

225–350 g (8–12 oz) farfalle –
  butterflies
salt
25 g (1 oz) butter
1 tablespoon oil
350 g (12 oz) button
  mushrooms, sliced

1 garlic clove, crushed
2 tablespoons chopped parsley
1 tablespoon lemon juice
freshly ground black pepper
grated Parmesan cheese,
  optional

Cook pasta in boiling salted water until just tender, drain well. Meanwhile, heat butter and oil in a large saucepan and fry the mushrooms and garlic for 4–5 minutes, until mushrooms are just tender. Remove from heat, stir in parsley, lemon juice and seasoning, then add this mixture to the hot drained pasta. Stir gently, to distribute ingredients, check seasoning. Transfer mixture to a hot dish and serve at once, sprinkled with grated Parmesan cheese if liked.

Farfalle with Courgettes, Peas and Mint

Fresh flavours and pretty colours are combined in this summery dish.

SERVES 4—6

225–350 g (8–12 oz) farfalle – butterflies
salt
25 g (1 oz) butter
1 tablespoon oil
450 g (1 lb) courgettes, thinly sliced

175 g (6 oz) shelled peas
2 tablespoons chopped mint
freshly ground black pepper
grated Parmesan cheese

Cook pasta in plenty of boiling salted water until just tender, drain thoroughly. While pasta is cooking, melt butter and oil in a large saucepan and cook the courgettes and peas over a gentle heat until tender: 5–8 minutes. Add courgettes and peas to hot drained pasta, together with fat from pan and chopped mint. Stir gently, add salt and pepper to taste. Spoon on to a hot dish, sprinkle with grated Parmesan cheese and serve at once.

Lasagne Baked with Aubergines, Onions and Tomatoes

A delicious colourful and welcoming dish that can be prepared in advance, then baked and served with a green salad or lightly cooked broccoli.

SERVES 4

350 g (12 oz) aubergines
salt
4–6 tablespoons oil
2 onions, sliced
175 g (6 oz) lasagne

350 g (12 oz) tomatoes, peeled
and sliced
125 g (4 oz) grated cheese
575 ml (1 pint) cheese sauce,
page 36

Peel aubergines, cut into thin rings, place in colander, sprinkle with salt. Leave for 30 minutes, then rinse, pat dry and fry in the oil until tender and lightly browned on both sides. Drain well on kitchen paper. Fry onions in remaining oil for 10 minutes. Cook lasagne as described on page 15. Set oven to 200°C (400°F), gas mark 6. Cover base of greased shallow ovenproof dish with lasagne, top with half the aubergine, onion and tomato, some grated cheese and cheese sauce. Repeat layers, then cover with lasagne, the rest of the cheese sauce and grated cheese. Bake for 45 minutes.

Lasagne and Brown Lentil Bake

This dish is tasty, filling and very cheap to make.

SERVES 4

175 g (6 oz) lasagne
salt
2 onions, chopped
1 stick of celery, chopped
1 carrot, finely chopped
2 tablespoons oil
225 g (8 oz) brown lentils,
   cooked, or 2 425-g (15-oz)
   cans

freshly ground black pepper
575 ml (1 pint) cheese sauce,
   page 36
50 g (2 oz) grated cheese,
   optional

Cook lasagne as described on page 15. Set oven to 200°C (400°F), gas mark 6. Fry onions, celery and carrot in the oil for 10–15 minutes, until tender and lightly browned. Drain lentils and add to vegetables, together with salt and pepper to taste. Put a layer of lasagne in a greased shallow ovenproof dish, cover with half lentils and a quarter of the sauce. Repeat layers, then cover with lasagne, remaining sauce and cheese if using. Bake for 45 minutes.

Quick Lasagne Bake

A quick and easy lasagne, excellent with a green salad.

SERVES 4

175 g (6 oz) lasagne
salt
450 g (1 lb) onions, sliced
2 tablespoons oil
450 g (1 lb) tomatoes, peeled and sliced, or a 425-g (15-oz) can, chopped

freshly ground black pepper
300 ml (11 fl oz) soured cream, natural yoghurt or cheese sauce, page 36
125 g (4 oz) grated cheese

Cook lasagne in plenty of boiling salted water as described on page 15. Set oven to 200°C (400°F), gas mark 6. Fry onions in the oil until tender: 10 minutes. Put a layer of lasagne in the base of a greased shallow ovenproof dish. Top with half the onion and tomato, season with salt and pepper, then sprinkle with a third of the grated cheese. Repeat these layers, then cover with lasagne. Spread soured cream, yoghurt or cheese sauce over the top, so lasagne is completely covered, sprinkle with remaining cheese and bake for 45 minutes.

Lasagne, Red Kidney Bean
and Wine Bake

Cheap to make, yet tasty enough for an informal supper party, served with remaining wine.

SERVES 4

175 g (6 oz) lasagne
salt
2 onions, chopped
2 tablespoons oil
225 g (8 oz) red kidney beans,
   soaked and cooked, or 2 425–g
   (15–oz) cans

225 g (8 oz) tomatoes, skinned,
   or a 225–g (8–oz) can
1 teaspoon ground cinnamon
2 tablespoons red wine
freshly ground black pepper
575 ml (1 pint) cheese sauce,
   page 36

Cook lasagne as described on page 15. Set oven to 200°C (400°F), gas mark 6. Fry onions in oil for 10 minutes. Drain kidney beans, chop tomatoes. Mix with onions, mashing beans. Add cinnamon, wine and seasoning. Put a layer of lasagne in a greased shallow ovenproof dish, cover with half red bean mixture and a quarter of the sauce. Repeat, then top with lasagne and remaining sauce. Bake for 45 minutes.

Lasagne with Spinach and Curd Cheese

SERVES 4

175 g (6 oz) lasagne
salt
450 g (1 lb) fresh or frozen
   spinach
225 g (8 oz) curd cheese
freshly grated nutmeg
freshly ground black pepper

For sauce
50 g (2 oz) butter
50 g (2 oz) flour
575 ml (1 pint) milk
125 g (4 oz) grated cheese
salt and freshly ground black
   pepper

First make sauce: melt butter in saucepan, add flour. Cook 1–2 minutes, add milk. Stir over heat until thickened, add cheese and seasoning. Cook lasagne as on page 15. Set oven to 200°C (400°F), gas mark 6. Wash fresh spinach, cook without extra water for 10 minutes; cook frozen spinach according to packet directions. Drain, chop and mix with curd cheese, grated nutmeg and salt and pepper. Cover base of greased shallow ovenproof dish with lasagne. Top with half spinach mixture, then a quarter of the sauce. Repeat layers, finishing with lasagne and remaining sauce. Bake for 45 minutes.

Lasagne with Mixed Vegetables and Basil

SERVES 4

175 g (6 oz) lasagne
salt
225 g (8 oz) onions, chopped
225 g (8 oz) carrots, finely diced
225 g (8 oz) leeks, shredded
225 g (8 oz) courgettes, thinly
  sliced
2 tablespoons vegetable oil
3 tomatoes, skinned and
  chopped

125 g (4 oz) button mushrooms,
  sliced
1 tablespoon fresh basil or 1
  teaspoon dried
freshly ground black pepper
575 ml (1 pint) cheese sauce,
  page 36
25 g (1 oz) grated cheese

Cook lasagne as on page 15. Set oven to 200°C (400°F), gas mark 6. Fry onions, carrots, leeks and courgettes gently in the oil, covered, for 20 minutes, stirring occasionally. Add tomatoes, mushrooms and basil, cook for 5 minutes. Season. Put a layer of lasagne in a greased shallow ovenproof dish, top with half vegetable mixture and a quarter of the sauce. Repeat, then cover with lasagne, rest of sauce and cheese. Bake for 45 minutes.

Macaroni with Butter Beans, Tomatoes and Black Olives

SERVES 4–6

225–350 g (8–12 oz) macaroni
salt
225 g (8 oz) butter beans, soaked
   and cooked, or 2 425–g
   (15–oz) cans
2 tablespoons olive oil

2 tablespoons lemon juice
350 g (12 oz) tomatoes, skinned
   and sliced
8–12 black olives
freshly ground black pepper
grated cheese, to serve

Cook pasta in plenty of boiling salted water until just tender, drain thoroughly. While pasta is cooking, heat butter beans in their liquid. Drain beans, add to hot drained pasta together with olive oil, lemon juice, tomatoes, black olives and salt and pepper to taste. Stir gently over the heat until ingredients are well distributed and piping hot, then serve immediately and hand round grated cheese separately.

Macaroni Cheese

This homely dish has the reputation of being stodgy and the reason, in my opinion, is that most recipes for it contain too much macaroni and too little sauce. This one is light and delicious.

SERVES 4

125 g (4 oz) macaroni
salt
40 g (1½ oz) butter
40 g (1½ oz) flour
575 ml (1 pint) milk

175 g (6 oz) grated cheese
freshly ground black pepper
50 g (2 oz) wholewheat
    breadcrumbs

Set oven to 200°C (400°F), gas mark 6. Cook macaroni in boiling, salted water until just tender, drain. Make sauce: melt butter in a saucepan, add flour, cook for a few seconds, then stir in a third of the milk. Bring to boil, stirring, then add another third of the milk and repeat until all milk has been added. Remove from heat, add macaroni, two-thirds of grated cheese and seasoning. Spoon into greased ovenproof dish, top with breadcrumbs and remaining cheese and bake for 40 minutes.

Macaroni with Four Cheeses

A classic dish that's really a sophisticated version of macaroni cheese. The point of interest is the inclusion of four different cheeses, each with its distinctive flavour and texture. I like this served with hot wholewheat toast and a green salad.

SERVES 4

125 g (4 oz) macaroni
salt
15 g (½ oz) butter
300 ml (½ pint) single cream
50 g (2 oz) grated Parmesan
  cheese
75 g (3 oz) Gruyère cheese,
  cubed

75 g (3 oz) provolone cheese,
  cubed
75 g (3 oz) mozzarella cheese,
  cubed
freshly ground black pepper

Cook macaroni in boiling, salted water until just tender, drain, return to saucepan and add the butter and cream. Turn mixture gently over the heat, then stir in half the Parmesan and all the other cheeses, season, and stir gently until the cheeses are heated through and beginning to melt. Sprinkle with remaining Parmesan and serve at once.

Macaroni Salad with Cheddar Cheese and Tomatoes

A colourful salad, excellent for lunch on a hot day, with some wholewheat rolls.

SERVES 4

225 g (8 oz) macaroni
salt
2 tablespoons olive oil
1 tablespoon wine vinegar
freshly ground black pepper

4 tomatoes
1 mild onion
175 g (6 oz) Cheddar cheese
crisp lettuce leaves
watercress

Cook pasta in plenty of boiling salted water until just tender; drain thoroughly. Put the oil and vinegar into a bowl with some salt and pepper and mix together. Add the pasta, turning it gently until coated with the dressing. Slice the tomatoes and onion, cut cheese into small dice or grate coarsely, and add these to the pasta. Mix gently to combine ingredients. Line a serving bowl or plate with lettuce leaves, spoon the pasta salad on top, then tuck some sprigs of watercress around the edge of the salad.

Macaroni and Curd Cheese Mould

I've included this dish because it is such an all-time favourite with my youngest daughter, especially if she can have a free hand with the tomato ketchup.

SERVES 4

125 g (4 oz) macaroni
salt
225 g (8 oz) curd cheese
125 g (4 oz) grated cheese

1 egg, beaten
freshly ground black pepper
wholewheat breadcrumbs

Set oven to 200°C (400°F), gas mark 6. Cook macaroni in boiling, salted water until just tender, drain and put into a bowl with the curd cheese, grated cheese and egg. Mix well, season to taste. Line a 450-g (1-lb) loaf tin with a strip of non-stick paper, grease generously with butter, sprinkle with wholewheat breadcrumbs. Spoon macaroni mixture into tin, smooth top. Bake for 45–50 minutes, until set and golden brown. Turn mould out on to warmed plate, and cut into slices to serve.

Ravioli with Cheese Filling in Tomato Sauce

SERVES 4

double quantity homemade
  pasta dough, pages 11–13
225 g (8 oz) curd cheese
75 g (3 oz) grated cheese
25 g (1 oz) grated Parmesan
  cheese

salt and pepper
1 egg, beaten
tomato sauce, page 51

Make pasta dough as described on pages 11–13, roll it into long pieces, place on lightly floured surface to prevent sticking. Mix together the curd cheese and grated cheeses and season to taste. Place small mounds of cheese mixture about 3 cm (1½ in) apart on half the pieces of pasta (see drawing on page 12), brush around each mound with beaten egg. Cover with rest of pasta, pressing down round edges and trying to exclude as much air as possible. Cut between the mounds with a pastry wheel. Put ravioli on a lightly floured surface and leave to dry for 30 minutes. Then put ravioli into a large panful of boiling salted water and cook for 4–6 minutes. Drain well, put on hot serving dish, pour hot tomato sauce on top.

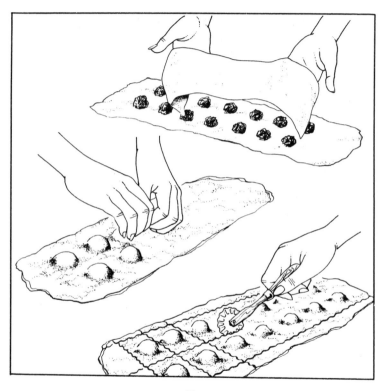

Ravioli with Curd Cheese and Hazel Nut Filling in Green Herb Sauce

SERVES 4

double quantity homemade
  pasta dough, pages 11–13
225 g (8 oz) curd cheese
1 garlic clove, crushed
100 g (4 oz) skinned hazel nuts,
  grated

salt and pepper
1 egg, beaten
150 ml (5 fl oz) single cream
2 tablespoons chopped mixed
  fresh herbs

Make pasta dough as described on pages 11–13, roll it into long pieces as in previous recipe and place on lightly floured surface. Mix together curd cheese, garlic, nuts and seasoning to taste. Place small mounds of curd cheese mixture about 3 cm (1½ in) apart on half the pieces of pasta, brush around each mound with beaten egg. Cover with rest of pasta, pressing down round edges and trying to exclude as much air as possible. Cut between the mounds with a pastry wheel. Leave ravioli for 30 minutes, then cook and drain as in previous recipe. Meanwhile heat cream and herbs in small pan, then pour over ravioli and serve.

Spaghetti with Aubergine and Wine Sauce

A colourful and rich-tasting sauce for spaghetti.

SERVES 4

1 large aubergine
salt
1 onion, chopped
2 tablespoons olive oil
1 garlic clove, crushed
1 green pepper, de-seeded and
  chopped
1 tablespoon chopped fresh basil
  or 1 teaspoon dried

225 g (8 oz) tomatoes, skinned
  and chopped
4 tablespoons red or white wine,
  whichever is available
freshly ground black pepper
225–350 g (8–12 oz) spaghetti
15 g (½ oz butter)
grated Parmesan cheese

Dice aubergine, sprinkle with salt, leave for 30 minutes to extract bitter juices, then rinse. Lightly brown onion and aubergine in the oil, then add the garlic, green pepper, basil, tomatoes and wine and cook gently for 25 minutes; season. Cook spaghetti as on page 51, drain, add butter, salt and pepper, serve with sauce, sprinkled with Parmesan cheese.

Spaghetti with Brown Lentil Bolognese

A very tasty vegetarian version of this classic dish.

SERVES 4

225 g (8 oz) brown lentils or 2
    425–g (15–oz) cans
2 onions, chopped
2 tablespoons oil
2 garlic cloves, crushed
2 celery sticks, chopped

2 carrots, finely diced
2 tablespoons tomato purée
salt and pepper
225–350 g (8–12 oz) spaghetti
15 g (½ oz) butter
grated Parmesan cheese

Cook dried lentils in plenty of water until tender: 45–50 minutes, then drain; or drain canned lentils. In either case, keep liquid. Brown onions in the oil, add garlic, celery and carrot; cover and cook gently for about 15 minutes, until tender. Add lentils, tomato purée, seasoning and a little reserved liquid to make thick soft consistency. Cook the spaghetti as on page 51, drain, add butter, salt and pepper. Serve spaghetti with sauce on top, sprinkled with Parmesan cheese.

Spaghetti with Lentil and Red Wine Sauce

Serve with rest of wine for a quick, cheap, informal supper with friends.

SERVES 4

1 onion, chopped
2 tablespoons olive oil
1 garlic clove, crushed
225 g (8 oz) tomatoes, skinned
  and chopped
175 g (6 oz) orange lentils
400 ml (15 fl oz) water
1 tablespoon chopped fresh basil
  or 1 teaspoon dried

4 tablespoons red wine
3 tablespoons tomato ketchup
salt and freshly ground black
  pepper
225–350 g (8–12 oz) spaghetti
15 g (½ oz) butter
grated Parmesan cheese

Fry onion in the oil for 5 minutes, then add the garlic, tomatoes, lentils and water and cook gently for 25 minutes. Stir in basil, wine, and tomato ketchup, simmer for 10–15 minutes, season. Cook spaghetti as on page 51, drain, add butter, salt and pepper, serve with sauce, sprinkled with Parmesan.

Spaghetti with Mushroom Sauce

This classic dish is usually made with double cream, but I prefer to make this lighter version using soured cream which has a third of the calories in double cream yet still gives a rich, smooth result.

SERVES 4

1 onion, chopped
40 g (1½ oz) butter
1 garlic clove, crushed
350 g (12 oz) button
  mushrooms, sliced
300 ml (½ pint) soured cream

salt and freshly ground black
  pepper
freshly grated nutmeg
225–350 g (8–12 oz) spaghetti
chopped parsley, to serve

Fry the onion gently in 25 g (1 oz) butter until softened: 10 minutes. Add garlic and mushrooms and cook gently for 4–5 minutes, then add soured cream. Remove from heat, season with salt, pepper and nutmeg, then leave on one side. Cook spaghetti as on page 51. Reheat sauce gently, stirring often. Drain spaghetti, add rest of butter, salt and pepper, tip on to hot dish, spoon sauce on top, sprinkle with parsley.

Spaghetti with Pesto

The classic way to serve spaghetti, bathed in this delectable green pesto sauce, wonderful as a first course or, with extra grated cheese and a salad, as a light main meal.

SERVES 4–6

2–3 garlic cloves, peeled
75 g (3 oz) fresh basil
75 g (3 oz) grated Parmesan
   cheese
25 g (1 oz) pine nuts

4 tablespoons olive oil
salt and pepper
225–350 g (8–12 oz) spaghetti
grated Parmesan cheese, to serve

The easiest way to make the pesto is to blend all the ingredients (except the spaghetti) to a purée in a blender or food processor. Otherwise crush the garlic to a paste with a little salt, using a pestle and mortar, then gradually add the rest of the ingredients, crushing and mixing to make a thick, smooth sauce. Cook spaghetti as on page 51, drain, return to pan. Add 2 tablespoons of boiling water to pesto, then add to spaghetti, stirring gently until spaghetti is green and glossy. Serve at once, with more Parmesan.

Spaghetti with Fresh Tomato Sauce

Particularly good made with wholewheat spaghetti and served with grated cheese and a green salad.

SERVES 4

225–350 g (8–12 oz) spaghetti
salt

grated Parmesan cheese, to serve
15 g (½ oz) butter

For the sauce
1 onion, chopped
25 g (1 oz) butter
1 tablespoon oil
1 garlic clove, crushed

700 g (1½ lb) tomatoes, skinned
and chopped
salt and freshly ground black
pepper

First make the sauce: fry onion gently in 25 g (1 oz) of butter and the oil until softened: 10 minutes. Add garlic and tomatoes, cook gently for 10–15 minutes, until pulpy. Season. Cook spaghetti in plenty of boiling salted water for 7–10 minutes, until just tender. Drain well, put back in pan with 15 g (½ oz) butter and some salt and pepper. Spoon spaghetti on to hot dish, top with sauce and cheese, serve at once.

Tagliatelle with Easy Cheese Sauce

Another example of a special pasta dish that you can rustle up in a moment; serve with a tomato and black olive side salad for an excellent quick supper.

SERVES 4–6

350 g (12 oz) tagliatelle
salt
15 g (½ oz) butter
150 ml (5 fl oz) single cream
175–225 g (6–8 oz) dolcelatte or
   Gorgonzola cheese, cut into
   rough dice

freshly ground black pepper
grated Parmesan cheese, to serve

Cook the tagliatelle until just tender in plenty of boiling salted water; drain well and put back in saucepan. Add butter, cream, cheese and a grinding of black pepper. Stir over a gentle heat until cheese has melted. Spoon on to a hot serving dish, or individual plates, sprinkle with Parmesan, and serve at once.

Tagliatelle with Roasted Peanut Sauce

SERVES 4–6

350 g (12 oz) tagliatelle
salt
15 g (½ oz) butter
225 g (8 oz) raw peanuts
4 tomatoes, skinned
125 g (4 oz) green pepper,
  de-seeded

125 g (4 oz) grated cheese
1 teaspoon chilli powder
275 ml (½ pint) milk
freshly ground black pepper

Cook tagliatelle, drain and add butter as described on page 52. Meanwhile roast peanuts by putting on dry baking sheet and placing under hot grill for a few minutes until nuts under skins are golden brown. Do not remove skins; put nuts into liquidizer or food processor with tomatoes, green pepper, cheese, chilli powder and milk and blend to a thick purée – you may need to do this in two batches. Transfer mixture to saucepan and heat gently, stirring. Thin with a little hot water if mixture seems too thick. Pile tagliatelle on to heated dish, pour sauce over and serve at once.

Tagliatelle Verde with Sweet Pepper Sauce

A pretty blend of colours: green tagliatelle with a vivid orange-red sauce. Serve with a green salad.

SERVES 4–6

1 onion, chopped
2 tablespoons oil
1 garlic clove, crushed
3 large red peppers, de-seeded and chopped
225 g (8 oz) tomatoes, skinned and chopped
2 tablespoons tomato purée
4 tablespoons dry sherry
salt and freshly ground black pepper
350 g (12 oz) tagliatelle
15 g (½ oz) butter
grated Parmesan cheese to serve

First make the sauce: fry onion gently in oil for 5 minutes, then add garlic and red pepper and cook for 10 minutes. Add tomatoes, tomato purée, sherry and seasoning and cook for a further 10–15 minutes. Cook tagliatelle in plenty of boiling salted water until tender; drain well and add the butter and some black pepper. Put tagliatelle on to a hot serving dish, spoon pepper mixture into the centre and sprinkle with grated Parmesan.

Tagliatelle with Walnut Sauce

This makes a delicious first course and is also good as a light lunch or supper dish, with a salad of watercress, apple and celery.

SERVES 4–6

350 g (12 oz) tagliatelle
salt
125 g (4 oz) walnuts
1 garlic clove, crushed

150 ml (5 fl oz) double cream
freshly ground black pepper
grated Parmesan cheese, to serve

Cook the tagliatelle until just tender in plenty of boiling salted water; drain well. While the tagliatelle is cooking, chop the walnuts very finely and put into a bowl. Add the garlic, cream and some salt and pepper and beat well to a smooth creamy consistency. If you've got a food processor, simply put all the ingredients for the sauce into this and blend for a few seconds until combined. Add this mixture to the hot tagliatelle, turning it with a fork until well coated. Spoon on to a hot serving dish or individual plates and serve at once.

Tortiglioni Salad with Avocado

Pasta spirals with buttery avocado make a good first course or summer lunch.

SERVES 4–6

225 g (8 oz) tortiglioni
salt
2 tablespoons olive oil
1 tablespoon wine vinegar
freshly ground black pepper
2 avocado pears

2 tablespoons lemon juice
½ small red pepper, de-seeded and chopped
4 spring onions, chopped
crisp lettuce leaves

Cook pasta in plenty of boiling salted water until just tender; drain thoroughly. Put oil, vinegar and some salt and pepper into a large bowl, add pasta, turning it gently until well coated. Leave until cool. Halve avocados, remove skin and stones, dice flesh, sprinkle with lemon juice. Add avocado to pasta, together with red pepper and onions, mix gently. Serve spooned on to a base of crisp lettuce leaves.

Tortiglioni with Garlic, Olive Oil and Fresh Herbs

Pasta spirals cook quickly and are excellent served simply like this, as a first course, or, with extra grated cheese and a juicy tomato and watercress salad, as a quick supper.

SERVES 4—6

350 g (12 oz) tortiglioni
salt
4 tablespoons olive oil
2 garlic cloves, crushed
3 tablespoons chopped fresh
  herbs

freshly ground black pepper
grated Parmesan cheese to serve,
  optional

Cook the tortiglioni in plenty of boiling salted water until just tender; drain into a colander. Put the olive oil into the pan in which the pasta was cooked, add the garlic and stir over the heat for a few seconds. Then add the drained pasta and stir gently until pasta is piping hot and the garlic and oil well distributed. Finally put in the herbs, stir again, and serve immediately, on hot plates, sprinkled with grated Parmesan if liked.

Vermicelli with Young Carrots, Broad Beans and Summer Savory

A delectable and pretty summer pasta dish. If summer savory isn't available, use other chopped fresh herbs or even chopped spring onions instead.

SERVES 4–6

1 onion, chopped
40 g (1½ oz) butter
1 tablespoon olive oil
225 g (8 oz) young carrots, finely diced
350 g (12 oz) shelled broad beans
salt and freshly ground black pepper

225–350 g (8–12 oz) vermicelli
2 tablespoons chopped summer savory
grated Parmesan cheese, optional

Fry the onion in the butter and oil for 5 minutes, then add the carrots and beans and cook gently, covered, for 10–15 minutes, until vegetables are tender. Season. Cook pasta in plenty of boiling salted water until just tender, drain thoroughly. Add the cooked vegetables to the cooked pasta, together with the summer savory. Mix gently, check seasoning. Serve at once, sprinkled with grated Parmesan, if you're using it.

59

Vermicelli with Chick Peas and Garlic

This traditional Italian dish, often called *tuoni e lampo* – 'thunder and lightning' – to describe the different textures of the pasta and the chick peas, is also good made with wholewheat pasta rings.

SERVES 4–6

225–350 g (8–12 oz) vermicelli
salt
225 g (8 oz) chick peas, soaked
   and cooked, or 2 425–g
   (15–oz) cans

3 tablespoons olive oil
2 garlic cloves, crushed
freshly ground black pepper
grated Parmesan cheese,
   optional

Cook pasta in plenty of boiling salted water until just tender, drain thoroughly. While pasta is cooking, heat chick peas in their cooking liquid. When pasta is ready, drain peas and add to pasta, together with oil and garlic. Stir gently over the heat until ingredients are well mixed, check seasoning, grinding in some black pepper, then spoon on to a heated serving dish, or individual plates, sprinkle with grated Parmesan, if you're using it, and serve immediately.

Index

63

64